THE

SEASONED

PERSONALITY

THE

*Seasoned**

PERSONALITY

Sara Kim

* a concept of personality that divides the year into two equal portions or seasons: SUMMER or WINTER.

ISBN:978-0-615-43233-5

Printed in the United States of America.

❖ *To my summer-born family* ❖

Table of Contents

CHAPTER

1

Introduction

HAVE YOU EVER WONDERED why you behave the way you do?

Have you ever thought why your family, your friends, and your co-workers act as they do?

Why do some people accomplish more than others?

We are all different individuals, but how many times do we really embrace someone who is different from us? We tend to see the world from our own point of view and often make less of the other person's perspective.

We may already know the strengths and weaknesses of our own personality, but may still struggle in our relationships with those around us. We tend not to accept those who are different from us.

Many times when we try hard to please others and to be accepted, we still find that we are often mistreated or, at least, misunderstood by people.

Why do humans behave the way they do?

What it is about me that cause others to treat me the way they do?

How can I understand the other person better?

How can I improve my social relationships?

People are seeking understanding, myself included. People go to seminars and therapy to learn about themselves so they can have better relationships. They spend vast amounts of time and money trying to find out how to live successfully with each other. Yet, as the old saying goes, none of us is perfect.

The human personality is a topic that has interested

people over many centuries. There have been a number of concepts, philosophies, and practices, mainly in the realms of psychology and psychiatry, developed to explain the traits or qualities that make up people's personalities.

In the fifth century B.C., the Greek doctor Hippocrates, known as the father of Western medicine, described four temperaments to categorize human personality: sanguine, melancholy, choleric, and phlegmatic. These simple categories were one of the first ways to look at human personality.

The Chinese horoscope has twelve symbolic animal signs, which depict a specific behavioral system, based on year of birth.

Psychiatrist Carl Jung, "the founder of analytical psychology," formed the concept of temperament—introversion and extroversion—through studying personality types. This concept was based on his observations.

In some parts of Asia, many people look at blood types such as type A and type B, to determine one's personality. For instance, during World War II, the Japanese military created army and navy fighting groups according to their blood type.[1]

Numbers of people often look at their daily horoscope to start, and, in many cases, guide their day.

Whether Chinese or Western astrology, your blood type, a form of modern psychology, or some other approach, *it is evident that people seek to learn more about their personalities,* and have been doing so throughout the history of our cultures.

---

[1] Gordon, Russell & Masao, Ohmura. "Blood types and athletic performance." *Journal of Psychology* 2002: 161–164.

In this book, I offer a new and easy-to-understand concept that is *another* valuable way to explain yours and others' personalities. It's called the "Seasoned" Personality.

L ET ME BEGIN by telling you how I came up with this concept of Seasoned Personality.

My interest in the Seasoned Personality started, in fact, with two American presidents. One day the question popped into my head: why do we celebrate only two presidents as a national holiday in America? That question led to the observation that both presidents were born in February. I began wondering why this month is so special and that prompted me to look up other presidents' birthdays.

I have always been an avid reader of biographies, with an interest in learning about the lives of the extraordinary individuals depicted in such books that mirrors my work and interest in the lives and problems of everyday people as a clinical social worker. Learning in biographies about how people lived in different ages and circumstances and with different gifts and challenges has fascinated me. I pay particular attention to birth dates. In fact, I have a photographic memory when it comes to birthdays,

This led to thinking about my family's, relatives' and friends' birthdays. I began looking over the birth dates of people from my past, as well as those of historically prominent persons.

I started compiling articles about people and events in their lives from newspapers and magazines. The more I gathered data, the more I realized that there were striking similarities between the behaviors of people who were born in either winter or summer months. There seemed to be a pattern developing.

I found this extremely interesting, and thus began my exploration into personalities as they relate to birth months. Over the years, I continued to investigate and gather more evidence and to observe people's general patterns of behavior to support my developing concept of the Seasoned Personality. I wanted to see if additional observations, carried out in the real world of people's lives in an unbiased form, would in fact corroborate the conclusions that I had made earlier.

In my professional career as a clinical social worker, I have worked with hundreds of clients who have different issues that cut across gender, race, and age. This clinical background also has enabled me to easily assess people's personalities and their needs.

As a result of working with clients, observing family and friends, and reflecting on my observations and research, I developed the concept that *the season in which a person is born has a major impact on one's personality.*

Rather than four seasons, my concept of the Seasoned Personality divides the year into two equal portions or seasons: **SUMMER** or **WINTER**. The season of birth greatly affects an individual's personality and helps explain one's behaviors and drive to accomplish.

Over the past decade, though not classifiable as a perfect system, my observations and conclusions have held true in the main.

How useful would it be to you to better succeed at relationships in your life, whether personal, familial, professional, scholastic or other? Knowing and understanding people is a key to success and to being happy.

In truth, anyone can use the concept of Seasoned Personality to identify the type of personality in front of them and to better understand people in general.

With the Seasoned Personality concept, you can also gain insight into people that you don't know, and possibly will never meet in your lifetime, but who nevertheless have some bearing on your existence, whether he/she is the president of your nation or the editor of your favorite magazine.

As you read this book, you will see references to strengths and weaknesses in winter- and summer-born people. None of this is information implies that a winter-born is better than a summer-born, or vice versa. These references are based on observational data. All descriptions are useful generalizations, naturally, since we can't make a perfect descriptive fit for every human being.

In *The Seasoned Personality*, the language is simple with no complex terminology. This book was not written for the scholastic elite or for the esoteric practitioner. It was written for anyone to read and use. The simplicity of this concept is predicated on the fact that a birthday is something that everyone remembers.

The Seasoned Personality is actually another means of seeing and predicting the nature and personality of people around us. None of what I am about to describe is based on semiotics, psychology, or celestial positions. Some readers might ask, "What's so different about this book compared to Western astrology?" Western astrology refers to the energy patterns of the planets in our solar system and their influence on human beings. My concept deals with seasons, especially two seasons, and is based on observation of behavior.

I wrote *The Seasoned Personality* to enable everyone who reads it to better understand and accept themselves and others just the way they are.

With that in mind, I hope that those of you who read *The Seasoned Personality* will find my conclusions not only interesting, but helpful to you and your relationships as you journey through this life.

CHAPTER

❖ 2 ❖

The Winter-Born

FOR MY THEORY and for the purpose of this book, the winter-born period consists of the months of **January, February, March** and **the early part of April**, as well as the **later part of October, November and December.**

The summer-born period consists of the months of **late April, May, June, July, August, September and early October.** August is a *hybrid* month, which means August-born can have both winter and summer qualities.

Take a moment to think about your own birth date and the birth dates of your family members, friends, or co-workers.

Are you a winter- or summer-born? What kind of a personality do you have?

Think of your different family members. Who is a summer-born? Who is a winter-born? Do you see any differences or similarities in their personalities?

Based on my findings, individuals who are winter-born, especially in the months of January, February, and March, are more *driven* and *focused* people.

People born during winter months are more likely to be:
Perfectionists
Persistent
Planners
Ambitious
Detail oriented
Well organized
Critical (of others and self)
Consistent
Strong willed
Self-driven
Highly motivated
Competitive
Analytical
Calculating
Multi-tasking
High achievers

Winter-borns are good at what they do, and they are very hard working. They often come across as uptight and narrow-minded and have a high expectation of themselves, as well as others.

Consider the birth dates of two of the most famous presidents of the United States; President Abraham Lincoln and President George Washington. Both men were born in February.

Historically, most presidents of the United States were winter-born. I will explain more about this in a later chapter. (Note: I chose presidents because we study them throughout our school life.)

Other famous people such as Ronald Reagan, Martin Luther King, Jr., J.R.R. Tolkien (author of the *Hobbit* and *Lord of the Rings* trilogy), Babe Ruth (legendary baseball player), and Oprah Winfrey, to name a few, were all winter-born.

It is amazing to note how many creative individuals such as inventors, musicians, and artists are born during winter months. In fact, Russian scientists reported that the majority of scientists and chemists in Russia were born during the winter months as compared to the summer months.[2]

I recently read a book called *My Disability, God's Ability*, by Dr. Young Woo Kang, who worked for President George W. Bush as an advisor for the National Council on Disability. I was moved by his determination even though he was blind. I began to think that the author had to be winter-born. Interestingly enough, when I researched him, I found out that his birthday was the same day as Dr. Martin Luther King, Jr.: January 15th.

I found myself intrigued with another individual not well known to everyone in our contemporary times. His name is Wilson Bentley—a man, who, during the era when photography as a subject was just coming out of its infancy, worked tirelessly to capture the image of a beautiful snowflake. He was the first person to photograph a single snow crystal in 1885.[3] He captured the images of more than 5000 snowflakes during his lifetime. He is remembered as "Snowflake Bentley," and he was born in February. He reflects the essence of winter-born individuals. They are **driven, persistent, and relentless** and are **perfectionists**, and

---

[2] Vinogradov, A.E. "Winter-biased birthday theory." *Scientometrics*. March 1998: 417–420.

[3] Martin, Jacqueline Briggs. *Snowflake Bentley*. Boston: Houghton Mifflin Co., 1998.

Wilson Bentley was all of this, and more, in his drive to achieve his goals.

You're probably already starting to ask yourself questions. You may be trying to figure out friends and family, and maybe even yourself. So, once again, I want to stress that when you view winter-borns, certain elements or traits tend to stand out versus other traits more typical of summer-borns. This does not mean that people born during one of these seasons are devoid of the other season's attributes, but each group manifests certain attributes more so than the other.

I also want to emphasize that as you read these descriptions, there is no intention to make the winter-born seem superior to the summer-born or the opposite. The winter-born have certain general strengths and weaknesses. The same goes for the summer-born.

It does not mean that the person born in winter will be more successful in life. Not at all. Winter-born people have certain personality characteristics that shine through, and in the same breath, summer-borns have theirs. So please, do not assume that I am weighing in on one season or the other. I have attempted to present this information in an objective and unbiased form.

CHAPTER

❖ 3 ❖

The Summer-Born

CONSIDER THOSE BORN IN late April, May, June, July, August, September, and early October as summer-born.

August people can go either way. They are people who have the winter-born traits and still have the summer-born's character. I consider August-born individuals as hybrids because this is the only month their personality can have a combination of summer and winter. In general, they can be very detail-oriented, yet at the same time easygoing.

I don't have an accurate reason as to why. My only explanation is that August is right in the middle of summer and winter. Even though August is considered a summer month, we know that summer will be coming to an end. In the United States, it's the month when we have to prepare for the fall, when many parts of American life—for example, school year, Congressional sessions, television programming—start a new cycle. This might be the reason that August-born may have the dual traits.

My study shows that the basic characteristics of summer-born individuals are:

Easy going
Nonchalant
Relaxed
More forgiving
Laid back
Considerate
Sensitive
Spontaneous
Idealistic
Inspiring
Sociable

> Flexible
> Daring
> Single-minded & single-tasking
> (as opposed to multi-tasking)
> Persistent (when they feel that a goal is important)
> Contented
> Charming
> And yes, very often stubborn.

IF YOU COMPARE that description to the winter-born, you will see distinct differences.

Nelson Mandela, a great leader who changed an entire nation, is an example of the summer-born. He became the president of South Africa after spending 27 years in prison because of his anti-apartheid activism. His mild manner, his patience, and his inspiration, while incarcerated for nearly three decades, helped to morph an entire nation from one where its indigenous peoples were treated like second-rate citizens to one where they are now on equal footing. This change launched Nelson Mandela as South Africa's first black president.

The 14th Dalai Lama was enthroned at the age of 15 as the spiritual leader of Tibet. That same year the People's Republic of China invaded Tibet and overthrew its governing body. The Dalai Lama eventually fled from Tibet a year later and set up a Tibetan government in exile in India. From there, he has been a potent spiritual leader and influence for the past five decades. He, too, epitomizes the summer-born. His leadership and peaceful approach have shown the strength of his inspiration, his forgiving attitude, and his sensitivity to the needs of the Tibetan people, who rely on his ability and spirituality. Finally, his single-mindedness has demonstrably shone through, as he has never given up.

Both leaders were born in July.

Both Nelson Mandela and the Dalai Lama embody those characteristics of the summer-born. Certainly, the strength of their personalities and attributes has made them very influential people. In their own way, they have helped to change our world for the better.

Yet another summer-born, Tim Russert, who anchored NBC's *Meet the Press,* was loved by the public. People viewed him as someone whom they could relate to. He was an humble man. Yet, there was no denying the fact he stuck to what he believed in. After his death, a colleague described how Tim did his homework when preparing for an interview and he would not compromise. He was a stubborn man who remained consistent in his belief and value system, especially about the importance of family. Tim's never-ending faithfulness to his hometown football team, the Buffalo Bills, was evident each time he chanted, "Let's go Buffalo!" on air. He was born in May.

It is also intriguing that many comedians are born in the summer. Dana Carvey and Bob Hope were born in June. Bill Cosby was born in July, and Adam Sandler in September. These summer-born individuals have a charm that draws people to them.

In my observation, you need summer-born people to be there to encourage you and to pull you through. They have a way of making things simple for one in a complicated world.

Yes, sometimes summer-borns have a tendency to be forgetful, clumsy, and disorganized, but they are always out there trying to work things out.

Summer-borns can become moody. On the other hand, when they are pushed into a corner they can become a tiger.

Summer-borns are also good Samaritans, willing to go out of their normal routine or comfort zone to help someone in need.

Where the winter-born can be considered "stuck up" and can be hard to compromise or reconcile with, the summer-born people are capable of smoothing things out. Watch a summer-born in action in a meeting or a confrontational situation.

Summer-borns have many friends and acquaintances. They also do not want complication in their lives.

Consider yourself after you have been through a cold winter. As soon as the first warm day appears, you want to "sing with the spring" and enjoy the outdoors in the sun. The rays of the warm sun and the fresh smell of clean air just make people want to see friends and enjoy the company of others and perhaps, to even be more kind to others.

Don't get me wrong. I'm not saying that the winter-born people are cold and heartless people. The winter-born can be very compassionate and giving. On the other hand, they are generally more focused and determined people.

The point, corroborated by my years of observation of people, is that both winter- and summer-borns are successful in their own right. They simply have different personalities.

Most certainly, if your partner was born in the other season, it would be wise of you to understand the differences in personality to make for smoother sailing in that relationship.

We need both summer- and winter-born people! We need to help, support, and enlighten each other. We need each other's strengths to work and live together harmoniously.

CHAPTER

4

This Could Be You

I WONDER IF YOU HAVE encountered any of these people. Can you guess their season of birth?

1. You arrange a carpooling schedule. When it's the other person's turn to pick up or drop off, she stops at the grocery store and doesn't bother calling.

2. Even though you're 80 years old, you go down to the basement to check on your daughter who has come to help you do the laundry because you want to make sure she's doing it correctly.

3. You forget to bring your music sheet to the chamber concert, so it delays the concert for 25 minutes. Everyone is waiting for you.

4. You ask many detailed questions when you're meeting with your financial advisor unlike other clients who say, "Oh, I trust you. I know you'll take good care of my investments."

5. Even though it's a simple question, you go on and on with detailed answers.

6. On the other hand, when asked what happened, you leave out most of the important information when answering questions. You love to answer with "good, it was fine," or "I don't know."

7. You show up late to work or appointments or gatherings.

8. You plan pretty much every aspect of your kids' lives by what time the kids should play, for how long, and with whom, with little flexibility.

9. People know you as a "control freak."

10. You cannot work if your desk or room is not clean.

11. You dump everything into your desk drawer instead of arranging it neatly.

12. You forget to pay your bills on time, and sometimes you leave your driveway with a coffee cup on the roof of your car.

These are just a few everyday examples that show some characteristic behavior of winter-born and summer-born.

Let's look at several in-depth everyday scenarios to illustrate differences in winter or summer-born personalities, and how they can markedly affect our relationships, and even our success.

Example #1

Jerry and Chloe have been married for several years. Jerry is a successful senior accountant. Chloe works in the marketing department of a large firm and is similarly very successful.

If you walked into their home, soon enough you couldn't help but notice some friction between them. You would find that Jerry harbors a degree of resentment and unstated upset over the fact that his wife is not well organized and that he has to pick up after her.

Chloe on the other hand would tell you that as much as she loves her husband, sometimes he's so anal-retentive about details and organizing things that she wants to scream and has done so on many occasions in the past. Not a few arguments have ensued over their differences in this regard.

If you chanced to open Jerry's walk-in closet, it would be neat to the very last shoe. The shirts, pants, and suits would not only be neatly hung, they might even be organized by color or type. Chloe's walk-in, on the other hand, would have shoes dropped in a disorderly fashion, not necessarily a mess or a heap, but certainly not with any apparent organization to them. The clothes would be hung or draped over hooks. On the floor would be found a number of purses and handbags still filled with contents that she had not yet bothered to go through, going back as far as a year or more.

Jerry's home office would be organized; his writing pad and pen would be arranged almost symmetrically. His favorite coffee mug would be centered on a place mat. His papers would be neatly stacked in a small filing rack. Chloe's portion of the home office would have a stack of papers, magazines and other things, including a calculator, several pens, and odds and ends, all piled in a tray. One or two half-full coffee cups or glasses would adorn one side of the desk.

Jerry's PDA would be meticulously organized with appointments and activities which he has already planned. Chloe, on the other hand, would be found trying to remember what appointment she had that day, and where she had put the piece of paper that she scribbled the appointment time onto the day before.

One personality is intensely organized and systematic in his approach to life; the other, casual and laid-back about things. Both are successful at what they do.

This isn't to say that Jerry is a better person than Chloe. This scenario isn't a measure of ability or virtues. It merely shows two very different personalities, and how they might clash on simple issues. Because they don't really understand the differences between each other, they do in fact clash repeatedly causing undue upset in their relationship.

Example # 2

Brett has recently finished getting his business degree and has landed a job as an account representative with a large company.

The company procedure is to set quarterly quotas for their reps, in terms of revenue from client accounts. Account reps, such as Brett, are expected to meet those goals, or at least come within ballpark range.

Within his first quarter, Brett has already fallen behind his quota. This is not because he hasn't worked hard and certainly not for lack of drive or ambition.

Brett enjoys working with his clients and loves the challenge of the chase when working on new accounts. He has, however, a disposition or tendency to leave things to the last minute and pile the details to one side.

His co-workers and clients enjoy his easy-going attitude. The latter enjoy his care and the fact that they can talk to him as their agent. However, at the end of the month, when account reports are supposed to be ready and turned into his supervisor, when paperwork for those new client companies is meant to be finalized and presented to the Accounting Department, and when numbers are up for review, Brett is found falling very short and scrambling.

He's left it all too late. He's procrastinated on the paperwork and administrative details, figuring that he can deal with it "later." In his forgetfulness, he comes in at the quarterly finish line with a poor showing, even though he's worked hard and actually opened up some new territory for the company.

He finds himself being reminded by his supervisor that he needs to buckle down on the details and get more diligent about following the administrative protocols of the company. He senses that his career with the firm is in jeopardy, if he doesn't change something.

Yet, statistically speaking, if a more thorough review of Brett's performance was done, it would show that he has the potential to start up more new client accounts than any other account rep. Because he has failed to deal with details, he looks like he's not performing well.

Example # 3

Emily is pulling up to the driveway of her mom's house on a Sunday afternoon; the same house that she grew up in. She is thinking how she'd like to turn around and go back to her apartment on the other side of town. She's not looking forward to spending the day here.

It's Thanksgiving and tradition dictates a yearly appearance on her part in the presence of the whole family—something that Emily dreads like the plague.

It isn't that Emily doesn't love her family. She does. But in her mind, if there is a more dysfunctional and mixed-up bunch of people on earth, she hasn't met them.

The problem is these family gatherings are painful and uncomfortable.

For instance, there is Aunt Sue—who insists on starting a debate over anything.

Uncle Bill puts a damper on anything really positive or upbeat and is confrontational. He constantly tries to remind everyone to "stay within reality," mostly because he's led a completely conservative, middle-of-the-road life and hasn't done anything marginally outside the box.

Between the two, one or both will eventually find a way to upset Emily's generally relaxed composure.

Younger cousin Stu, who usually appears so casual and calm, somehow manages to regularly lose either his job or his girlfriend, or both. He ends up venting his frustrations to the whole family.

Then there is Grandma who has the ability to talk incessantly. So much so that Emily eventually can be found trying to hide in a quiet corner of the house to avoid the salvo avalanching from her mouth, until she can safely slip out the front door and head home for the night.

To top it all off, there is Mom, the "drill sergeant" of family gatherings.

"Everybody stay out of the kitchen, I'm cooking," she can be heard barking out at anyone who comes near.

"Ok—dig in and eat—*COME on!*" She then orders the rest of the family to the table and stands there with her hands on her hips as everyone obediently complies.

"I'll just take care of these dishes now." Mom would be found jumping up and whisking away the plates out from under people's noses even before they were fully done eating.

Emily had watched the same performances play out, year after year, like a Broadway show. Family members were characters acting parts with perfection, as if they had rehearsed the piece and performed it a dozen times before. And in fact, they *had*.

Emily parks her car, takes a deep breath, and prepares for "The Family Gathering."

Do any of these scenarios sound familiar to you?

Even if they don't, you will surely have your own similar experiences. Unless you live on the dark side of the moon, you are interacting with people day-in and day-out, and you will have your own stories to tell.

When you analyze these scenarios from the viewpoint of winter- and summer-borns, you can better understand the issues that played out. This also helps us to understand relationship problems.

N THE FIRST example, Jerry is a winter-born. His wife, Chloe, is a summer-born. Jerry is driven, while his wife is laid-back and relaxed. This causes certain stress-points between them. If you compare Jerry to the attributes in the winter-born chapter, you see that Jerry is a planner. He's organized. He's a perfectionist. Chloe, on the other hand, is easy-going. She's an idealist who's charming with people, but she doesn't pay attention to the same details or organization that Jerry does.

In the second example, Brett, the new upstart at the firm, is a casual, relaxed guy. He is a summer-born. He has ambition, he has drive, but he tends to be lax when it comes to details and organization. His strengths are that he is an idealist, he is good with people, and he is contented and forgiving. These qualities make him a good salesman. Yet because he isn't detail oriented, he generally doesn't do well with paperwork. He has weakness in organizational skills.

In the last example, you have a salad-bowl of personalities. Emily is a summer-born. Her mother, a winter-born, is passionate and driven about everything, including cooking, and fully commands the family gathering. The other personalities present are a mix of the two seasons. Her aunt and uncle are winter-borns, while her cousin Stu and her grandmother are summer-borns. These differences create an interesting push and pull, as the family personalities interact with one another.

Everyone has strengths and weaknesses. Their combination, along with our basic nature and temperament, are what makes each of us unique and individual.

The point here is that there are personality differences between a summer- and winter-born. The people in the case studies above are not recognizing those differences, whether in themselves or others. If they did, they could learn how to reconcile their issues.

To give an analogy, if you know that a grizzly bear is going to snap at your head if you walk into its cave after a long hibernation, you simply understand that it's best to stay out. That little piece of understanding leads to a longer, happier life. If you don't know that, and happen to wander in and start up a conversation with that hungry bear and lose your head in the process, you cannot really blame the bear. You should have known better. Life with others is no different.

Because people are so different, the more we understand each other, the easier it is to succeed in our lives with one another.

CHAPTER

❖ 5 ❖

Explanation

WHY DO WINTER- AND summer-borns have different personalities? I base my concept primarily on observations through the years.

However, as I read various books and articles, I came upon some findings that offered explanations about seasonal factors that could affect personality development.

There are scientific studies that look at personality traits and birth month. A Japanese study done in 2008 focused on what effect the month of birth had on personality traits of healthy Japanese. The study showed that a higher ambient temperature at birth month related to higher scores when measuring self-directness and persistence in adult females.[4] Here, the study relates to the effects of temperature on personality traits. Its finding helps confirm my observation that summer-born are more single-minded and persistent.

A recent study by Harvard University professor Jerome Kagan explains that a contributing factor to one's personality may come from "the month you were born, not, as astrology would have it, because of the alignment of planets, but because a pregnant mother's hormones influence a baby's nervous system development and these alter with the changing seasons."[5]

After reading about these scientific studies, I began thinking about what reasons, based in nature, might have influenced seasonal personality.

In the past in many areas of our world, where the days of sunlight were shorter and longer nights existed, people were required to work harder and faster to accomplish their

---

[4] Mitsuhiro Kamata., et al. "Effect of month of birth on personality traits of healthy Japanese." *European Psychiatry* March 2009: 86–90.

[5] Kagan, Jerome. *The Temperamental Thread: How Genes, Culture, Time and Luck Makes Us Who We Are.* Washington, D.C.: Dana Press, 2010.

survival needs in a much shorter time period. There was less time to waste or play around. When the weather permitted them to farm or build houses, people had to get to work fast to accomplish essential tasks and to prepare for the long months of limited or no sunlight.

In contrast, in countries or cultures closer to the equator, where far fewer light limitations exist, survival demands were not influenced as much by this factor. People are generally more relaxed about getting things done to accomplish their needs throughout the year.

Another factor I considered in the differences between a winter-born and summer-born could be a person's mood. Mood changes in the context of environmental changes. In the northern hemisphere, the winter months are cold and dark. People don't move around a lot. They tend to stay inside their home, reading, and talking with family. They may become somewhat melancholy and pensive. People tend to think and plan for the coming springtime and warm summer months.

The summer months, however, tend to bring about opposite changes in a person's mood. The bright and warm days make people more relaxed and outgoing. They tend to spend more time outdoors, being active.

One research study describes how the season of birth of an individual affects mental health, with affective disorders occurring more frequently in people born during the winter months.[6] In general, I observed that the winter-born tend to be more moody and self-critical, in part because of their drive toward high goals.

---

[6] Murray, Gregory. *Seasonality, Personality and the Circadian Regulation of Mood.* New York: Nova Science Pub. Inc., 2006.

But, whether these two factors contribute to my concept, I conclude, based on my own observations, that those who are born in winter tend to have a greater expressed tendency to *need to get things done* before the daylight is over. Those who are born in summer tend to relax a little bit more because of longer daylight.

ALTHOUGH THE SCIENTIFIC studies lend weight to my theory of the Seasoned Personality, the purpose of this book is to offer a different concept of understanding personalities according to season. To me, the Seasoned Personality is observable. Just like the effects of gravity are observable.

We don't have to know *why* gravity works to know *that* it works. We cannot see gravity with the eye. But we certainly *can* sense it and feel its influence on our lives every minute of the day.

My contention is that, although not yet scientifically explained, a person born in the winter generally will have personality traits that are different than the summer-born.

Naturally, we could also consider other environmental or circumstantial influences. These cannot be disregarded in personality development. But nevertheless, they do not change my general observations.

For example, if you were born into a family where both of your parents were winter-borns, even though you're a summer-born, you could take on the characteristics of a winter-born just by the dominating and continuous influence of your parents.

Let's consider other environmental factors or circumstances. For example, because of a family's economic situation, a young boy or girl may have had to work earlier as a teenager to help support the family. As a result, he or she learned to be diligent, responsible, and hard working. This economic influence applies regardless of which season they were born.

Other factors such as sibling order (eldest child being responsible for the other siblings) can play into one's developing personality. We've all seen this: an older brother or sister takes on the leadership role or role model, becomes accustomed to delegating and organizing, and the younger siblings tend to fall in line.

Culture, gender, economic status, life experiences, religious beliefs, friendships and relationship, innate intellectual ability—all may have a part influencing personality, in addition to season of one's birth.

❖ 6 ❖

When Presidents Were Born

I MENTIONED EARLIER THAT one of the major factors that launched me onto this course of research was the observation that two of the most influential presidents of our nation, George Washington and Abraham Lincoln, were both born in the month of February.

If my observations about the season of birth are correct, it is a worthy task to look at leaders of our nation, potential leaders, or leaders anywhere.

This is no attempt to imply that season of birth is a criteria for selection of leaders. There is no slightest illusion that a president, or any leader, is better if they are winter-born or summer-born.

Although many of you are aware of the names of our current and past presidents, more than likely you don't know their birth months. Let's look at our presidents and see when they were born and see how the Seasonal Personality is reflected in their actions and leadership of the country.

January

Millard Fillmore (1-7-1800)
William McKinley (1-29-1843)
Franklin D. Roosevelt (1-30-1882)
Richard Nixon (1-9-1913)

February

George Washington (2-22-1732)
William Henry Harrison (2-9-1773)
Abraham Lincoln (2-12-1809)
Ronald Reagan (2-6-1911)

March

James Madison (3-16-1751)
Andrew Jackson (3-15-1767)
John Tyler (3-29-1790)
Grover Cleveland (3-18-1837)

April

Thomas Jefferson (4-13-1743)
James Monroe (4-28-1758)
James Buchanan (4-23-1791)
Ulysses S. Grant (4-27-1822)

May

Harry S. Truman (5-8-1884)
John F. Kennedy (5-29-1917)

June

George H. W. Bush (6-12-1924)

July

John Quincy Adams (7-11-1767)
Calvin Coolidge (7-4-1872)
Gerald R. Ford (7-14-1913)
George W. Bush (7-6-1946)

August

Benjamin Harrison (8-20-1833)
Herbert Hoover (8-10-1874)
Lyndon B. Johnson (8-27-1908)
Bill Clinton (8-19-1946)
Barack Obama (8-4-1961)

September

William Howard Taft (9-15-1857)

October

John Adams (10-30-1735)
Rutherford B. Hayes (10-4-1822)
Chester A. Arthur (10-5-1829)
Theodore Roosevelt (10-27-1858)
Dwight D. Eisenhower (10-14-1890)
Jimmy Carter (10-1-1924)

November

James Knox Polk (11-2-1795)
Zachary Taylor (11-24-1784)
Franklin Pierce (11-23-1804)
James A. Garfield (11-19-1831)
Warren G. Harding (11-2-1865)

December

Martin Van Buren (12-5-1782)

Andrew Johnson (12-19-1808)

Woodrow Wilson (12-28-1856)

WHAT CONCLUSIONS can we make?

Which presidents were considered better leaders than others and what were their birth months? Many presidential historians differ in their opinion about who they think are the greatest presidents. We can form our opinions based on our values and priorities.

Out of the 44 presidents, there are 26 presidents who were born in the winter.

The month of October has the most—six. October-born people have leadership qualities. They are not as "intense" as the winters (January, February, and March), and not as "easygoing" as the summers (June and July). This can be a good combination when it comes to accomplishing work and relating to people.

Theodore Roosevelt, who was sworn in as the youngest president due to President McKinley's assassination, left a legacy, including the Nobel Peace Prize, which he won for mediating the Russo-Japanese war. Jimmy Carter also won the Nobel Peace Prize. Dwight Eisenhower's campaign slogan was "I like Ike." These examples of October-born characteristics show how likable and approachable these men were.

You can see that their personalities coincide with the month they are born. (See the previous chapters on characteristics).

After examining this data, you can ask some obvious questions:

Do *you* think that having a summer-born president is better than having a winter-born?

In your opinion (even though some of us might not be familiar with presidents such as John Tyler, Calvin Coolidge, William Taft, Warren Harding), which presidents accomplished more while they were in office?

Lastly, which presidents do we remember the most? Which presidents do you admire? In what month were they born? Can you see now why some winter-born presidents or summer-born presidents accomplished things the way they did while they were in office?

Month by Month

AS I MENTIONED EARLIER, I kept records for over a decade, compiling them according to people's birth months. Initially, I planned to verify my theory of the two seasons. Over time I saw the need to explain the Seasoned Personality month by month. I discovered that people born in each month express their own degree of summer or winter's general characteristics.

The following insights are based on my contacts and observations of numerous personalities of people, including clients, friends, family members, and public figures that I read about and saw on television.

In this chapter, you will find for each month a list featuring a selection of well-known figures of the past, as well as contemporary artists, politicians, and other influential people. You will also find a short biography of selective people who depict the characteristic of that particular month. Each biography focuses mainly on accomplishments, which I think reflect the attributes of the winter- or summer-born's personality. I am sure there are other famous people whom I have left out. It's not that I didn't choose *you* as an example. I just couldn't find all of you!

As you read these names, you might smile and say, "Aha!"

Think about the characteristics of winter- and summer-borns as you go over these lists.

For example, Serena Williams (September-born) has been characterized as single-minded in her pursuit of athletic experience. Vincent Van Gogh (March-born) was known to have periods of depression or melancholy.

January

♦ **Benjamin Franklin:** Writer, printer, publisher, scientist, diplomat, revolutionary, inventor and philosopher. Some of his inventions include the lightning rod, bifocals, and the Franklin stove. Daylight Saving Time was first conceived by Benjamin Franklin. He is well-known for publishing *Poor Richard's Almanac.*

♦ **Martin Luther King Jr.:** Baptist minister and social activist who led the civil rights movement in the United States from the mid-1950s until his death by assassination in 1968. His leadership was fundamental to that movement's success in ending the legal segregation of African-Americans in the South and other parts of the United States. He was the youngest person ever to win the Nobel Peace Prize.

♦ **Elvis Presley:** He was known as the king of rock 'n' roll. Despite many failures making soundtracks and Hollywood films, he returned and was rewarded by multiple successful tours. He also won the Grammy award three times and received the Grammy Lifetime Achievement Award.

♦ **Oprah Winfrey:** Oprah is a talk show host, philanthropist, producer, and actress. Although she experienced hardships as a child, she has been respected by many for overcoming adversity to become a benefactor to others. She is considered the most influential woman in the world.

◆ **Muhammad Ali:** Ali is known as one of the greatest heavyweight boxers of all time. At the 1960 Summer Olympics in Rome, Muhammad won the gold medal in the light heavyweight division and he also won the heavyweight championship three times for the first time in history.

◆ **Jackie Robinson:** He was the first African-American to play Major League Baseball. In 1949, Robinson won the National League Most Valuable Player Award, the first black person to do so. Robinson was inducted into the Baseball Hall of Fame in 1962, and in 1997, the MLB retired his number (42). After his death, he was awarded the Congressional Gold Medal and the Presidential Medal of Freedom.

Alice Paul (women's rights activist)

D.W. Griffith (TV personality)

J.D. Salinger (writer)

J.R.R. Tolkien (author of The Hobbit and Lord of the Rings trilogy)

Louis Braille (inventor of the Braille system for the blind)

Joan of Arc (warrior and saint)

Katie Couric (TV personality)

George Foreman boxer)

John Hancock (statesman who helped spur the American Revolution)

Julia Louis-Dreyfus (actress)

Jim Carrey (actor)

Kevin Costner (actor)

Edwin "Buzz" Aldrin (astronaut; he and Neil

Armstrong were the first men to land on the moon)

Mary Lou Retton (gymnast)

Virginia Woolf (writer)

Vince Carter (basketball player)

Wolfgang Amadeus Mozart (legendary composer of classical music)

Cuba Gooding Jr. (actor)

Justin Timberlake (singer)

Alicia Keys (singer)

Mel Gibson (actor/director)

Paul Newman (actor)

Rush Limbaugh (radio talk show host)

David Bowie (singer)

Nicholas Cage (actor)

Rod Stewart (singer)

Wayne Gretzky (Hall of Fame hockey player)

Attributes

The January-born carry the "winter-born" traits down to the bone. They are determined, hardworking, and driven. They are often charismatic and can be good leaders.

They can sometimes be somewhat negative, even though they come across as pleasant people. By negative, I mean they are critical of themselves and others.

February

Langston Hughes (poet)

Norman Rockwell (artist)

Babe Ruth (baseball player)

Chris Rock (comedian/actor)

Greg Norman (golfer)

Michael Bloomberg (N.Y. City mayor)

George Harrison (musician and member of the legendary Beatles band)

Nolan Bushnell (inventor of Pong and founder of Atari)

Thomas Edison (inventor of the electric light bulb and more)

Steven Jobs (innovator of personal computers and the IT world)

Susan B. Anthony (civil rights activist)

Rosa Parks (civil rights activist)

W.E.B. DuBois (writer)

Langston Hughes (American poet and novelist)

Charles Lindberg (famous pilot—first solo flight across the Atlantic Ocean)

Garth Brooks (singer)

Jennifer Aniston (actress)

John Travolta (actor)

Drew Barrymore (actress)

Chelsea Clinton (President Clinton's daughter)

Lisa Marie Presley (singer)

Boris Yeltsin (former President of Russia)

Farrah Fawcett (actress)

Ashton Kutcher (actor)

Paris Hilton (actress)

Michael Jordan (basketball player)

Attributes

See chapter nine for a more in-depth look at February-born individuals.

March

♦ **Albert Einstein:** He was an intellectual genius whose intelligence made him one of the most well known scientists and people in history. He won the 1921 Nobel Peace Prize for his discovery of the photoelectric effect. Today, people regard him as the father of modern physics.

♦ **Sandra Day O'Connor:** She is well known for being the first woman on the Supreme Court; she was the Associate Justice from 1981 to 2006. On the 2004 list of the most powerful and influential women, she was surpassed only by Hillary Clinton, Condoleezza Rice, and Laura Bush.

♦ **Theodor Geisel "Dr. Seuss":** Seuss was a children's book author whose numerous books gained him his national popularity. Some of the books are *The Cat in the Hat, How the Grinch Stole Christmas*, and *Horton Hears a Who*. He also won the Academy Award for Documentary Feature for his film *Design For Death* for the U.S. Animation Department.

♦ **Gloria Steinem:** She was a journalist who was nationally recognized as the leader of the women's liberation movement in the 1960s-'70s. Steinem continually pursued her dream of liberation for women, received multiple awards, and founded many organizations and projects.

♦ **Alexander Graham Bell:** Bell became famous when he invented the telephone in 1876. Not only did he work on telecommunication, he also worked on aeronautics. On February 14, 1876, he raced Elisha Gray to the patent office to file his patent. The race paid off and Bell was credited with the invention of the telephone.

♦ **Jackie Joyner-Kersee:** She was one of the greatest women athletes in America. She won three gold medals, one silver medal, and two bronze medals in the 1984 Los Angeles, 1988 Seoul, 1992 Barcelona, and the 1996 Atlanta Olympics. She, along with other great athletes like Tony Hawk, Muhammad Ali, and Lance Armstrong, founded Athletes for Hope.

Ron Howard (movie director)
Jon Bon Jovi (singer)
Johann Sebastian Bach (composer)
Fryderyk Chopin (composer)
Joseph Haydn (composer)
Vincent Van Gogh (painter)
Shaquille O'Neal (basketball player)
Michael Eisner (CEO of Disney)
James Taylor (singer)
Jason Kidd (basketball player)
Mariah Carey (singer)
Jennifer Capriati (tennis player)
Queen Latifah (rapper/actress)
Reese Witherspoon (actress)
Sharon Stone (actress)
Peyton Manning (football player)
Celine Dion (singer)
Carrie Underwood (singer)

Al Gore (former Vice President)
Nancy Pelosi (House Speaker)
Cy Young (baseball player)
Eva Longoria Parker (actress)
Rupert Murdoch (CEO & Chairman of News Corp)

Attributes

Just look at the names of these people! Most of these people made and changed history. As you can see, they worked hard for their accomplishments. Their characteristics are intensity, driven, competitiveness, efficiency, detail-oriented, and a "never give up" attitude.

The March-born can be negative at times. Because they have a high expectation for themselves, they expect others to do the same. They might not always be the most popular among their acquaintances. In their view of things, their way is the best way, and you can't stop them.

April

♦ **Wilbur Wright:** He was one of the two brothers who were credited with the creation of the first successful airplane. They owe their success to their constant work with machinery like bicycles, motors, and many others. In late 1903, the Wright brothers kept on trying new ideas to create the airplane.

♦ **Maya Angelou:** She is an autobiographer who was active in the Civil Rights Movement. Angelou is the author of *I Know Why the Caged Bird Sings*, but some of her books were deemed to be controversial and are banned in certain schools. She also was the first poet to recite a poem at a president's inauguration (Bill Clinton) since Robert Frost at John F. Kennedy's inauguration.

♦ **Leonardo da Vinci:** The most accurate way to describe da Vinci is a Renaissance man, a man who excels at all things. He often experimented with different styles of painting and also devised plans for a helicopter, a tank, and much more. He also painted the Last Supper and the Mona Lisa.

♦ **Charlie Chaplin:** Chaplin was one of the best known actors of the silent film era. He wrote and directed his films and also composed the music for them. He made and was a part of countless films that gave comic relief to those who needed it.

Hans Christian Anderson (classic Danish author)
Colin Powell (former Secretary of State)
Russell Crowe (actor)
Kofi Annan (former UN secretary general)
Kareem Abdul-Jabbar (basketball player)
Queen Elizabeth II of Great Britain
Barbra Streisand (singer)
Jack Nicholson (actor)
William Shakespeare (playwright)
Chipper Jones (baseball player)
Jay Leno (TV personality)
Andre Agassi (tennis player)
William Randolph Hearst (businessman)
J. Robert Oppenheimer (inventor)
Heath Ledger (actor)

Kirsten Dunst (actress)

David Letterman (TV personality)

Susan Boyle (singer)

Alec Baldwin (actor)

Marlon Brando (actor)

Jennifer Garner (actress)

Conan O'Brien (TV personality)

Al Pacino (actor)

Robert Downey Jr. (actor)

Attributes

The April-born are very good with people, sometimes too good. They tend to flatter their way to achieve their personal objectives. They can be very chameleon-like and are charismatic and strategic about how they go about things.

Even though some can be efficient and driven, they might not necessarily have those intense winter-born characteristics, especially those born in the latter part of April.

Interesting Note

Did you know that four of the most popular talk show hosts of contemporary times were born in April? Consider **David Letterman** on the *Late Show with David Letterman*, **Jay Leno**, who has hosted *The Tonight Show* for seventeen years, **Conan O'Brien** on *Late Night with Conan O'Brien*, and **Jimmy Kimmel** on *Jimmy Kimmel Live*.

They're all funny, articulate, witty, and able to make their guests feel comfortable, whether or not

> they like the guests personally. They know how to deal with people. That's one of the big characteristics of the April-born.

May

♦ **John Paul II:** John Paul II was the pope of the Catholic Church from 1978-2005. He gave the title "blessed" to 1340 people and gave the title of saint to 438 clergy members because of his belief that everyone is called to be holy. He was also firm in his Orthodox Catholic beliefs.

♦ **Martha Graham:** Martha Graham was a pioneer in the field of modern dance. She used new techniques to show the feelings of life: anger, joy, and passion. She is the only dancer who received the Medal of Freedom.

♦ **Rachel Carson:** Rachel was a marine biologist who pushed forward the environmental movement. She wrote a trilogy that describes marine life throughout the ocean. She determinately exploited the problems on the environment by pesticides which led to the ban on DDT.

♦ **Madeleine Albright:** She was the first woman Secretary of State with a vote count of 99-0. Throughout her life she obtained numerous honorary Doctors of Law from many different colleges. She also is fluent in a number of languages.

♦ **Malcolm X:** He was an African-American civil rights activist who was also a member of the Nation of

Islam and later became a Sunni Muslim. His racial experiences shaped his life. He gave hundreds of speeches and actively pursued what he believed in.

James Brown (singer)
George Clooney (actor)
Johannes Brahms (composer)
George Lucas (filmmaker)
Naomi Campbell (model)
Rudolph Giuliani (former New York mayor)
Walt Whitman (poet)
Sally Ride (first female astronaut)
Jim Thorpe (Olympic medalist)
Tony Blair (former Prime Minister of England)
David Beckham (soccer player)
Tim Russert (political analyst)
The Rock (wrestler)
Billy Joel (songwriter)
Bono (singer)
Janet Jackson (singer)
Malcolm X (civil right activist)
Mike Myers (actor)
Brooke Shields (actress)

Attributes

They are mellow and easygoing on the surface, but they are very strong willed and uncompromising when it comes to something they believe in strongly. If they think they're right, they really don't listen to you. They can also be somewhat selfish and are usually single-minded about things.

May birth individuals can be the nicest people in the world and are very popular because of their positive make-up.

June

♦ **Helen Keller:** She was a women's right activist who was both deaf and blind. She wrote books about her life as a deaf and blind person and how she learned to communicate with the world by using sign language.

♦ **Margaret Bourke-White:** Bourke-White was an American photographer who is most known for being allowed to take pictures of the Soviet Union. She became the first woman to cover war and fighting in combat zones.

♦ **Wilma Rudolph:** She was an American track star who, up until the age of 12, had to wear a leg brace to support her twisted leg due to polio. She went on to win 3 Olympic gold medals in the 1960 Rome Games.

♦ **Bob Hope:** Hope was a comedian who was well known for his humanitarian efforts. He was named the only honorary veteran of the U.S. military.

♦ **Frank Lloyd Wright:** He was a famous architect who completed more than 500 works and designed more than a thousand projects in his lifetime. He experimented with many different types of buildings like skyscrapers, hotels, and churches to name a few.

Dana Carvey (comedian)

Angelina Jolie (actress)

Anna Kournikova (tennis player)

Steffi Graf (tennis player)

Venus Williams (tennis player)

Paul McCartney (singer)

Nicole Kidman (actress)

Carson Daly (TV personality)

Derek Jeter (baseball player)

Babe Didrikson Zaharias (first female golfer)

Natalie Portman (actress)

Ashley and Mary-Kate Olsen (actresses)

Prince William of Great Britain

Toby Maguire (actor)

John Cusack (actor)

George Pataki (former NY governor)

Kanye West (singer)

Johnny Depp (actor)

Attributes

They seem relaxed and content. People born in the month of June have a good sense of humor. They generally have a good relationship with others. People find them to be down to earth and pleasant.

They can also be too easygoing and lax about things. They might not be the most organized people, and as a result they can frustrate those who are more organized in their approach. However, they are responsible for their work and quite successful at what they do. Most importantly, it's their personable attitude that wins people's heart.

> ## Interesting Note:
>
> We see many athletes born in this month. Three famous female tennis players were born in June, as well as Olympic runner Wilma Rudolph.

July

◆ **John D. Rockefeller:** He was the founder of Standard Oil Company, became the world's richest man and the first American billionaire. He donated a large sum of money that was important in the eradication of both malaria and hookworm.

◆ **J.K. Rowling:** Rowling is most well known for the creation of the Harry Potter series, which made her one of the richest women in Britain. Her story of how she started off as an extremely poor woman to an international celebrity is equally famous.

◆ **Thurgood Marshall:** He was the first African American to become a member of the Supreme Court. One of his most famous cases was Brown versus the Board of Education, which he won. He was given the Presidential Medal of Freedom by Bill Clinton.

◆ **Henry Ford:** Ford was credited with the creation of the assembly line and the mass-produced Model T automobile. He thought that the key to global peace is consumerism, which led to many technological advancements on his part.

♦ **Amelia Earhart:** She was the first woman to fly across the Atlantic Ocean solo. She even attempted to circumnavigate the globe until her famous disappearance happened in the Pacific. She also founded the 99s, an organization of female aviators.

Tom Cruise (actor)
Neil Simon (playwright)
Michelle Kwan (figure skater)
Tom Hanks (actor)
Bill Cosby (comedian)
Nelson Mandela (anti-apartheid leader)
Barry Bonds (baseball player)
Alex Rodriguez (baseball player)
Beatrix Potter (author)
Peter Jennings (anchor)
Arnold Schwarzenegger (former actor and Governor of California)
Liv Tyler (actress)
Jessica Simpson (singer)
Harrison Ford (actor)
Lil' Kim (rapper)
Daniel Radcliffe (actor)
Kelly Clark (snowboarder)
David Hasselhoff (actor)
Jennifer Lopez (actress)
Sandra Bullock (actress)
Ernest Hemingway (author)

Attributes

Those born in July are predominantly unassuming, laid back individuals. They come across as very peaceful and content, as well as charming! They are sentimental, caring, and find it hard to let go of things. They come across as nonchalant and not worried about things. They like to please people and play "politically correct."

They can be *very* sensitive to criticism and tend to procrastinate when making decisions. They tend to like everything and everyone. Yet, they can also sometimes have a hard time moving on with things.

I read an article about Jessica Simpson having a breakdown due to her beloved dog being killed by a coyote. That story illustrates how a July-born can have a hard time letting go of things and how loving and caring they can be.

August

♦ **Wilbur Wright:** He was the driving force to accomplish what their dream was. He took the initiative by using singular pronouns to describe their accomplishments. See **Orville Wright.**

♦ **Neil Armstrong:** He was the first person ever to step on the moon and for this he received the Congressional Space Medal of Honor. He was also a member of the U.S. Navy during the Korean War.

♦ **William Clark:** He was an explorer who traveled the Louisiana Territory to the Pacific Ocean to document what he saw. It took him and **Meriwether Lewis** two years to come back to the U.S. He was

63

named governor of Mississippi and Lewis was appointed governor of the Louisiana territory.

♦ **Mother Teresa:** She was a nun who founded an organization called Missionaries for Charity, which gave free services to the poor and needy, and is still active today. She devoted her life to helping the needy and the afflicted.

♦ **John McCain:** He was the United States senator of Arizona for four terms and will be running for a fifth term. He was a prisoner of war, captured by the North Vietnamese, until 1973, and he also ran for president against Barack Obama and against George W. Bush to be the Republican candidate.

Meriwether Lewis (expeditionary) see William Clark
Tom Brady (football player)
Jeff Gordon (auto racer)
Patrick Ewing (basketball player)
David Robinson (basketball player)
Whitney Houston (singer)
Pete Sampras (tennis player)
Fidel Castro (president of Cuba)
Halle Berry (actress)
Sean Penn (actor/director)
Madonna (singer/actress)
Connie Chung (journalist)
Cal Ripken Jr. (baseball player)
Regis Philbin (TV personality)
Michael Jackson (singer)
Elisha Graves Otis (inventor)
Charlize Theron (actress)

Ben Affleck (actor)
Edward Norton (actor)
Matthew Perry (actor)
Kobe Bryant (basketball player)
Cameron Diaz (actress)

Attributes

As mentioned in Chapter 3, August-born people can have characteristics of winter or summer. They tend to possess the best of both worlds. Because of this, they can be described as hybrids. This may be a reason why one of our recent presidents, Bill Clinton, and our current president, Barack Obama, are often described as very personable and popular, but they also get the work done very proficiently!

September

♦ **Lance Armstrong:** He is a cyclist who won the Tour de France seven consecutive times even after having cancer. He had tumors in his brain and lungs but still recovered from it.

♦ **Andrea Bocelli:** He was a blind singer who recorded 14 studio albums and seven of his albums have topped the classical album charts, a record. He is one of the greatest Italian classical singers in the world.

♦ **Milton Hershey:** He founded the Hershey Chocolate Company and the town of Hershey, Pa. He tried to open candy parlors in Philadelphia and New York, but both failed. He eventually bought acres of land and began mass-producing milk chocolate, which was a luxury product.

♦ **Jane Addams:** She was the first woman to receive the Nobel Peace prize. She directed people's attentions to the problems of mothers around the country, like meeting the needs of their children.

♦ **Jim Henson:** He was the creator of the Muppets and he also made some characters in Sesame Street and Star Wars, like Yoda. He was originally going to be a Christian scientist but went on to direct movies and television shows.

♦ **Jesse Owens:** He was a track and field Olympian who won four gold medals in the Berlin Olympics of 1936. Adi Dassler, the founder of Adidas, made Owens the first sponsored African-American player.

Mike Piazza (baseball player)
Charlie Sheen (actor)
Jesse James (outlaw)
Adam Sandler (actor)
B.B. King (blues musician)
Will Smith (actor)
Serena Williams (tennis player)
Gwyneth Paltrow (actress)
Catherine Zeta-Jones (actress)
Bryant Gumbel (TV personality)
Martina Hingis (tennis player)
Rosie Perez (actress)
Prince Harry of Great Britain
Faith Hill (singer)
Pink (singer)
David Souter (Supreme Court justice)
Beyonce Knowles (singer)

Bruce Springsteen (singer)

Attributes

September-born are compulsive individuals. If they have a desire to do something, they have to do it right away. They can come across as being very stubborn about the things they want to accomplish. They are very focused on one goal. When they are working on that goal, they can be unstoppable. They are always full of new ideas!

They can also be laid back and easygoing. They're not always the most organized people, and sometimes they can be wishy-washy. Because of their easily approachable attitudes, people find them likable.

October

- ◆ **Hillary Clinton**: She is the 67th U.S. Secretary of State and a former First Lady to Bill Clinton. She also sat on the board of directors for various corporations, including Walmart.

- ◆ **Bill Gates**: He is the founder of Microsoft Software Company and of the Bill and Melinda Gates Foundation, which donates money to charities and to scientific research. He is the youngest self-made billionaire in history.

- ◆ **Juliette Low**: Low was the founder of the American Girl Scouts. Although early in her life she was captured by Native Americans, she kept an upbeat personality. She was very eccentric and even stood on her hands to show off her shoes

♦ **Maya Lin:** She was an architect who designed the Vietnam War Veterans Memorial in Washington D.C. She beat out more than a thousand other applicants to design the monument.

♦ **Noah Webster:** He was a lexicographer who led the production of educational books that taught people to spell, read, and the correct way to use grammar that emphasized Christian values. He also attempted to set up several schools, which failed.

♦ **Eleanor Roosevelt:** She was the wife of Franklin D. Roosevelt who worked for equal rights for women. She also was instrumental in the passing of the New Deal coalition.

Billy Graham (preacher)
Sting (singer)
Vladimir Putin (politician)
John Lennon (musician)
Paul Simon (songwriter)
Ichiro Suzuki (baseball player)
Midori (violinist)
Chuck Berry (songwriter)
"Jelly Roll" Morton (musician)
Mae Jemison (first woman of color to go into space)
Jonas Salk (developed a vaccine to prevent polio)
Kate Winslet (actress)
Matt Damon (actor)
Usher (singer)
Sarah Ferguson (British royalty)
Eminem (rapper)
Julia Roberts (actress)

Julie Andrews (actress)

Mahmoud Ahmadinejad (President of Iran)

Pablo Picasso (painter)

Arthur Miller (author)

Attributes

October-borns tend to have leadership qualities similar to April-borns. They are ambitious and competitive. But they can also be envious of others.

People who are born in the beginning of October have summer-born characteristics. Those born in the middle to the end of October, carry the winter-born characteristics.

Interesting Note:

The very first woman to practice law before the United States Supreme Court and to appear on a presidential ballot was born in October. Her name is Belva Ann Bennett Lockwood, born October 24, 1830.[7]

Interestingly, former N.Y. Senator and current Secretary of State Hillary Clinton was also born in October (10-26-1947).

Finally, out of the forty-four U.S. Presidents, more were born in October than any other month.

---

[7] Bolton, Ralph. Personal Interview. 22 Nov. 2008.

November

♦ **Willis Carrier:** He is the father of modern air conditioning. He started up multiple businesses in New York, but none worked until Newark, NJ. The company slowed down during the two World Wars, but his corporation bounced back.

♦ **Marie Curie:** She was a French physicist and chemist who was well known for the discovery of two new elements: polonium and radium. She also was the first person to win two Nobel Peace Prizes.

♦ **Shirley Chisholm:** She was the first African-American to become a presidential candidate for a major party. She was first elected to the New York State legislature and then to the House of Representatives.

♦ **Georgia O'Keeffe:** She was a well-known still life artist who painted rocks, bones, landscapes, and most notably, flowers. She also was known for bringing American styles of art to Europe in a time when Europe was influencing America.

♦ **Mark Twain:** Mark Twain was an American author who specialized in satire. He wrote *The Adventures of Tom Sawyer* and *The Adventures of Huckleberry Finn*. He was an imperialist, pacifist, and he believed in emancipation and setting slaves free.

♦ **Billie Jean King:** She was a former professional tennis player who advocated against sexism in professional sports. She also beat 55-year-old Bobby Riggs in the "Battle of the Sexes."

Laura Bush (first lady)
Bryan Adams (singer)
Condoleezza Rice (secretary of state)
Ken Griffey Jr. (baseball player)
Caroline Kennedy Schlossberg (President Kennedy's daughter)
Jon Stewart (TV personality)
Mariano Rivera (baseball player)
Benjamin Banneker (inventor)
Claude Monet (painter)
Phil Simms (football player/sportscaster)
Ethan Hawke (actor)
Sean "Puffy" Combs (rapper/businessman)
Leonardo DiCaprio (actor)
Whoopi Goldberg (actress)
Ben Stiller (actor)
Meg Ryan (actress)
Miley Cyrus (singer/actress)
Jodie Foster (actress)
C. S. Lewis (author)

Attributes

November-born people begin to show the somewhat intense winter-born traits. They are efficient, organized, and driven. They can be very loyal. The best way to describe the November-born is that they are very diplomatic.

While they are generally good workers, they can be somewhat negative and critical of themselves and others. They tend to be melancholy.

December

♦ **Emily Dickinson:** She was a poet who lived a very inclusive life, who was reluctant to greet guests; when she did communicate, it was through correspondence. She was a very private poet, so only about a dozen of her 800 poems were published during her lifetime.

♦ **Ludwig van Beethoven:** He was a German composer and pianist who was considered to be one of the most influential composers of all time. He also continued to work even after he lost his hearing.

♦ **Steven Spielberg:** He is an American film director who directed some of the best known films of the modern era: *ET, Schindler's List, Saving Private Ryan, Jaws,* and *Jurassic Park,* to name a few. He also helped to found DreamWorks.

♦ **Walt Disney:** He was considered to be one of the greatest film producers in history. He dreamed up Mickey Mouse and won 26 Academy awards and was nominated 59 times. He was the inspiration for many places and things such as Disneyworld, the Disney Channel, and the Magic Kingdom.

♦ **Eli Whitney:** He was an inventor who created the cotton gin, a device that removed cotton fibers from cottonseeds with minimal effort. This actually strengthened the slave industry, but his original intent was to harm the industry.

♦ **Clara Barton:** She was a nurse who founded the American Red Cross. She served during the

American Civil War and helped wounded people on some of the grimmest battlefields.

Bette Midler (singer/actress)

John Kerry (U.S. senator)

Diane Sawyer (TV journalist)

Cokie Roberts (TV journalist)

Denzel Washington (actor)

Tiger Woods (golfer)

John Jay (first Chief Justice of the Supreme Court)

Clarence Birdseye (inventor, Quick Freeze Machine)

Andrew Carnegie (industrialist)

Britney Spears (singer)

Jamie Foxx (actor)

Ray Romano (comedian)

Ricky Martin (singer)

Jude Law (actor)

Val Kilmer (actor)

Attributes

All of these listed have the qualities of winter-borns. They are successful and good at what they do. They are quite efficient, organized, and self-motivated. They are all about detail, detail, detail!

People born in December tend to be sensitive and somewhat negative. Because of their high expectations of themselves, sometimes they drive themselves crazy.

B UT DON'T JUST TAKE my word about these month-by-month attributes.

Look at your own list of people from your life. Look at the winter-borns that you know. Do their personalities match up more or less to the months described above? What about the summer-borns in your life? Do you see parallels?

What about you? Which month were you born in? Do the above attributes describe your general personality?

Remember the characteristics capture general personality.

Trying to put everyone into a neat little box, with a "one-size-fits-all" label doesn't work, because people are too varied and too individual to ever do that.

But in terms of a general description of patterns or traits, I hope you find the above month-by-month analysis to be useful.

Just for your curiosity, I have listed some infamous persons:

Dictators

Adolf Hitler—April 20

Joseph Stalin—December 18

Napoleon—August 15

Mussolini—July 29

Fidel Castro—August 13

Saddam Hussein—April 28

Mao Zedong—December 26

Kim Il Sung—April 15

Murderers

Charles Manson—November 12

The Menendez Brothers- Joseph Lyle (January 10), Erik Galen (November 27)

Susan Smith—September 26

Traitors

Benedict Arnold—January 14

General Armstrong Custer—December 5

❖ 8 ❖

The February-Born

IN THE PROCESS OF DOING my research, I noticed there were many famous people born in February, including athletes, composers, writers, conductors, Olympic medalists, scientists, actors and politicians who were born in this month. This was fascinating to me.

In *Time* magazine (February 16, 2009), historian Henry Louis Gates Jr. mentioned that the month of February is the darkest, coldest, and shortest month in reference to its being Black History Month. In contrast, I find this cold month to be very special. It's interesting that we celebrate Valentine's Day (love), Ash Wednesday (atonement), and Presidents' birthdays (contribution and accomplishment) all in one month.

As I began my research by looking at the February-born, I was bombarded by the number of famous people born in this month. Read over this list (in chronological order by year of birth) to discover how special this birth month is.

1595
Galileo Galilei (scientist invented the telescope)
1572
Hans Christopher Haiden (composer)
1637
Toyotomi Hideyoshi (unified Japan)
1685
George Frederic Handel (German composer)
1723
Tobias Mayer ("Method of Lunars"
for longitude determination)
1732
George Washington (1st U.S. president)

1743

Luigi Boccherini (Italian composer, cellist)

1773

William Henry Harrison (9th U.S. president)

1802

Victor Hugo (French author)

1807

Henry Wadsworth Longfellow (poet)

1809

Abraham Lincoln (16th U.S. president)

Charles Darwin (Evolution author)

1810

Frederic Chopin (Polish composer)

1812

Charles Dickens (novelist)

1817

Frederick Douglass (first high ranking black
in U.S. government)

1820

Susan Brownell Anthony (women's suffragette)

1821

Elizabeth Blackwell (physician/first woman
to gain MD in U.S. Founded London School of Medicine
for Women, 1875)

1834

Dmitri Mendelejev (Russian chemist—
devised Periodic Table)

1837

Sir James Augustus (created Oxford Dictionary)

1838

Margaret Knight (inventor—"The female Thomas Edison")

Pierre Jules Cesar Janssen

(discovered hydrogen in Sun)

1847

Thomas Edison (inventor)

1852

Charles Taze Russell (founded Jehovah's Witnesses)

1857

Lord Baden-Powell (founded Boy Scouts)

Heinrich Hertz (physicist, 1st to broadcast

& receive radio waves)

1859

Sholem Aleichem (Jewish author whose stories became

Fiddler on the Roof)

1867

Laura Ingalls Wilder (author of *Little House on the Prairie*)

1868

Constance Gore-Booth Markiewicz (Irish patriot and

playwright—first woman elected to British Parliament)

1870

Alfred Adler (psychiatrist—Inferiority Complex)

1878

Hattie Wyatt Caraway (first woman to be elected

to U.S. Senate)

1879

Charles Follis (first black U.S. football player)

1890

Boris Pasternak (Russian novelist—*Dr. Zhivago*)

1895

Babe Ruth (greatest baseball player)

1898

Fritz Zwicky (Swiss astronomer—Super Nova)

1902

John Steinbeck (Nobel Prize author)

Charles Lindbergh (aviator/made first solo airplane flight across the Atlantic)

1906

Clyde William Tombaugh (astronomer—discovered Pluto)

1910

Lee Byung Chul (Korean industrialist/founder—Samsung)

1911

Ronald Reagan (40th U.S. President)

1912

Byron Nelson (PGA golfer—won 19 tournaments in 1945)

1913

Rosa Parks (civil rights activist)

Jimmy Hoffa (Union leader)

1917

Sidney Sheldon (author)

1921

Hugh Downs (TV journalist)

1922

Joeri Averbach (Russian chess grandmaster)

1923

Mary Elizabeth "Liz" Smith (gossip columnist)

1927

Sidney Poitier (actor)

1928

Ariel Sharon (11th Prime Minister of Israel)

1931

James Dean (actor)

Isabel Peron (dancer/42nd president of Argentina)

1932

Edward Moore "Ted" Kennedy (former senator D-MA)

Elizabeth Taylor (actress)

Johnny Cash (singer/songwriter)

1933

Yoko Ono Lennon (artist/musician, Mrs. John Lennon)

1934

Ralph Nader (attorney/political activist)

1935

Sonny Bono (singer)

1938

Judy Blume (writer)

1940

Tom Brokaw (news anchor)

Ted Koppel (newscaster)

1941

Naomi Uemura (mountain climber—

first Japanese to scale Everest)

1942

Joe Lieberman (Senator—D-CT)

Kim Jong Il (dictator of North Korea)

1943

George Harrison (Beatles singer/guitarist)

1944

Carl Bernstein (*Washington Post* reporter,

broke Watergate story)

Jerry Springer (talk show host)

1950

Mark Spitz (swimmer—won seven gold medals
in the 1972 Olympics)

1955

Greg Norman (championship golfer)

John Grisham (writer)

Steve Jobs (co-founder of Apple Company)

1959

John McEnroe (tennis champ)

Lawrence Taylor (NFL's greatest linebacker (NY Giants))

1960

Jim Kelly (NFL Quarterback (Buffalo Bills))

Tony Robbins (motivational speaker/author)

1961

George Stephanopoulos (news anchor)

1963

Vijay Singh (professional golfer)

Michael Jordan (basketball champ)

1964

Sarah Palin (former Governor of Alaska)

1965

Michael Dell (CEO of Dell)

1966

Cindy Crawford (super model)

1972

Michael Chang (tennis star)

1973

Chris Robinson (NBA guard)

1981

Josh Groban (singer/songwriter)

1994
Dakota Fanning (actress)

Aren't you impressed with the list? I was.

MY ANALYSIS OF THESE PEOPLE who were born in the month of February shows that they were *driven* to succeed in their life's walk.

Many of them were/are movers and shakers. They are people from all walks of life. Many of them were pioneers and innovators. Some are known for serving others and being positive role models. One is famous for being a dictator (Kim Jong Il of North Korea.)

Their lives show that they are persistent, driven people. Those of us who have had relationships with people who are often called "driven" know that they can be difficult to live with as far as interpersonal relations are concerned. As the saying goes, it is "their way or the highway."

In 2009, we celebrated Abraham Lincoln's 200th birthday. It is said that there's no other person, beside Jesus Christ, about whom people have written more books. President Lincoln was described as "Skillful in analysis, discerned with precision the central idea on which a question turned. He reasoned clearly, his reflective judgment was good and his purposes were fixed."[8] He is the classic example of a February-born.

Two years ago *Newsweek* magazine (July 14, 2008) ran a cover story featuring Lincoln vs. Darwin. They were both born on February 12, 1809.

---

[8] Schauffler, Haven, ed. *Lincoln's Birthday*. New York: Moffat, Yard and Co., 1914.

Smithsonian magazine (February 2009) also featured both men as "Their genius, their legacies, their humanity . . . they changed the world forever." This article confirmed my belief that Lincoln was an extraordinary man.

It's also very interesting to see that four famous television news anchors were all born in February—Tom Brokaw, Hugh Downs, Ted Koppel, and George Stephanopoulos. In comparison, four of the most famous talk show hosts were born in April—as noted in the section under April.

Perhaps February people are good orators (for example, Abraham Lincoln and Ronald Reagan). They are persuasive, convincing, and articulate. Numerous acclaimed authors were also born in February.

We also find that many famous women, especially those associated with the women's rights movements, were born in February.

In addition, a number of February women were first in their fields. These include: the first woman to be elected to the U.S. Senate (Hattie Wyatt Caraway), the first woman to earn an MD (Elizabeth Blackwell), and the first woman to be elected to the British Parliament (Constance Gore-Booth Markievicz).

Of all ladies born in February, the most famous is Rosa Parks.

ROSA PARKS, AN AFRICAN-AMERICAN woman, lived in an age and time in the American south when black people were rated as second-class citizens. They were required to sit in the back of buses, attend only black segregated schools, and suffered other severe violations of their human rights. In

1955, Rosa Parks refused to give up her seat on a bus to a white person. Her act of quiet defiance became symbolic in the efforts against racial segregation. She became an African civil rights activist, collaborating with Martin Luther King, Jr. in the drive for civil rights of African-Americans.

Because of her unyielding persistence and belief, Rosa Park's actions help lay the groundwork for the United States to elect the first black American president in 2008, only fifty-three years after she first stood up and said "NO."

Jim Kelly, Hall of Fame football player, and his son, Hunter, were born on the same day (February 14). Hunter Kelly had a rare disease called globoid-cell leukodystrophy (Krabbe disease). It is an inherited enzyme disorder that affects 1 in 100,000 children born in the United States. A child who is diagnosed with this disease has a few months, perhaps one or two years to live. Hunter died at the young age of eight, but is believed to be the oldest person to have lived this long with Krabbe disease. His doctor described Hunter as a "brave and tough kid." Jim Kelly and his wife devoted their time and energy to Hunter, and created the Hunter's Hope Foundation. Most certainly, the Kellys have been and are a great example of February-born driven people.

Another example I recently discovered: during the U.S. Open semi-final tennis match between Rafael Nadal, world number one player, and Mikhail Youzhny, the NBC commentator Dick Enberg mentioned Nadal's coach, his uncle Toni. Enberg quoted from a *New York Times* article (September 10, 2010) that Toni Nadal is a tough disciplinarian and is the one who helps Rafael to be grounded and humble. In one incident, Nadal, his uncle, and his publicist,

Benito Pérez-Barbadillo, decided to have dinner at a restaurant in Shanghai. Toni noticed his nephew was not wearing a jacket, and there was a dress code. Rafael's publicist told him the restaurant would probably bend the rule. But Toni Nadal said, "Rafael, you must go change."

When I heard that story, I said to myself, "Toni Nadal has to be a February-born!" When I checked his birthday, I was elated to discover it was February 21. Toni is described as down-to-earth and level-headed. He believes that only with hard work you can improve your life and he always tries hard to improve. That is the perfect description of February-born. I should give him the nickname of "Lexus" because the company's motto is "The Relentless Pursuit of Perfection."

It is worth mentioning again the story of Snowflake Bentley, as this man epitomizes the energy and passion of the February-born.

WILSON BENTLEY WAS BORN February 9, 1865 in Jericho, Vermont. Home-schooled until he was fourteen years old, Wilson read all the encyclopedias at home. He was an inquisitive kid, who loved the outdoors and developed a fascination for snow crystals. By the time he was fifteen, he had already drawn a hundred snow crystals each winter for three consecutive years. His parents eventually bought him a camera, which cost them a herd of ten cows. In the book *Snowflake Bentley*, author Jacqueline Briggs Martin wrote, "When he found only jumbled, broken crystals, he brushed the tray clean with a turkey feather and held it out again. He waited hours for the right crystal. Some winters he was able to make only a few dozen good pictures. Some winters he made hundreds."[9]

Willy died of pneumonia after walking six miles home through a blizzard in 1931. He had published 49 popular books and 11 articles about snow crystals, frost, dew and raindrops.

I first read the book about him when our first child was six years old. I remembered then and there that I wanted to write a book about February-borns. I would have loved to meet Mr. Bentley. His devotion, dedication, persistence, stubbornness, and hard work in producing photographs of a beautiful snow flake make him truly Mr. February!

At this point you are probably asking, "Why February?" Well, I have always been intrigued by February-born individuals, especially when it comes to their zealousness toward what they do. However, I never imagined the amount of information I would find when I started writing this section of the book. I was just amazed at the names of the people who were born in February.

All the years of speculation and observation I had about February-borns were confirmed by these findings.

Yes, I do wonder too, 'Why February? What is so special about them?

This question remains unanswered at this time. Possibly in the future, we will have an answer for it. And in case you were wondering, I am a February-born!

---

[9] Martin, Jacqueline Briggs. *Snowflake Bentley*. Boston: Houghton Mifflin Co., 1998.

CHAPTER

❖ 9 ❖

Recommendation

N THIS FINAL CHAPTER, I ask you the reader to take a big step back for the purposes of objectivity and perspective.

Think about someone in your life whom you don't completely understand or with whom you are having problems. Maybe it's a difficult relationship. Maybe it is your wife, maybe your husband. Maybe it's your boss, your teacher, your closest friend, or maybe... it's you!

Look at this person from the perspective of *The Seasoned Personality.*

First, is he or she (or you) a winter-born or a summer-born?

If that person was born between January through the early part of April, including late October, November and December, they are a winter-born.

If they were born in the later part of April through early October, they are a summer-born.

Remember, the month of August can sometimes be a hybrid of the two seasons.

Next, what attributes would you look for in that person? Let's say that you've established that your boyfriend (or girlfriend) is a winter-born:

- ♦ Is he/she persistent and strong-willed? (summer-born can have this)

- ♦ Is he/she highly motivated and driven to the point that sometimes it annoys you?

- ♦ Is he/she detail-oriented, organized or a perfectionist?

- ♦ Does he/she all too-often seem critical of others as well as himself?

♦ Is he/she a multi-tasker?

You may not instantly see every quality standing out like a bright light. But if you look carefully at him/her, you will see characteristics that parallel these strengths and weaknesses in the winter-born personality.

Now, if you see them, don't be critical. Don't hang onto any negative aspects. To do this, you really have to stay objective without any slant or bias. What do you SEE?

People sometimes look at something or someone and see what they want to see or what they THINK they see as opposed to just LOOKING. For instance, one person sees a dog walking down the street and thinks how they'd love to get one just like that one. Another person sees the same dog and instantly thinks of the time they were bitten by one as a child and cringes and thinks that all dogs are dangerous. It's the same with people. We sometimes get impressions, instantaneous ideas, or fixations, and we lose sight of really what is there in front of us.

Once you've established what character you CAN see in your boyfriend (as an example), you have now reached a better understanding of him. What you do with that is entirely up to you. But when you understand your boyfriend better, you can then begin to appreciate him for who he is. Because of this, you'll probably find yourself more tolerant, more at peace, and less inclined to react negatively to him.

Understanding is a very potent tool.

Remember the example I gave earlier in this book about the hungry bear? If you walk into a bear's cave and wake it up after months of hibernation, you're quite likely to lose your head. You may deserve this for not taking a moment to look at what is in front of you. But if you acknowledge the

94

fact that it is hungry and dangerous in that state, feed the bear, and keep your distance, then your chances of survival are sufficiently improved.

People aren't bears, but the analogy serves to press home the point, know your people.

If, for example, you are a parent, and your thirteen-year-old daughter is being very lax and nonchalant about her school work, then take a look at her. She's quite possibly a summer-born. You could argue with her. Ground her. Cut off her social life, take away her iPod and cell phone and make her miserable. Or you could simply understand her better through a grasp of the personality traits of the summer-born. You could recognize that because of who she is, she will sometimes seem laid-back in her approach in getting things done. That does not mean she will not get things done or not follow the timeline you want. You just have to come to terms that she operates in different way.

If you as the parent are a winter-born, then you are possibly seeing life through a *different* intensity of personality traits. It isn't at all that you're better and your daughter is worse. It simply means that, in general, your strengths and weaknesses as a person weigh in heavier on certain qualities whereas hers tip the scales another way. Neither person is better. But recognition of each other's personalities can help both sides to relate to each other better and to succeed.

To resolve this, first understand your daughter better as a summer-born, then help her. Rather than getting exasperated by her behavior, help her by making a planner, creating charts to assist her to navigate her way successfully, and giving her ample time to get ready in the morning. Try to instill more motivation to do her homework in order to achieve higher grades and to maintain a focus on her goals within the reality of what must be accomplished, without at the same time crushing her self-determinism.

In another possible scenario, what if you are the owner of a construction company and every day when you walk through the job-site, you observe one of your foremen being very demanding of his crew. He is insisting that the men pick up the pace by ordering them around. This foreman is very detailed about things and is being overly critical about the men's work standards. The workers are grumbling about this guy and are not happy. News reaches your desk, asking you to do something about the situation, as good workers are threatening to leave.

What do you do? Do you just fire the foreman, and find someone that is able to run the site without generating worker-upset? That wouldn't exactly be a basis for dismissal, yet you have to do something.

What if you called the foreman on the carpet and confronted him with the various reports about the workers being upset and complaining? What if you told him to lighten up? Maybe that would work. Or maybe the foreman would just feel confused or upset, or he'd go back and really take his feelings out on the workers for getting him in trouble with the boss.

If you studied your foreman with the Seasoned Personality in mind, you would see that he is a winter-born. He's driven, intense, he's detail oriented, and he's systematic and organized. He's a perfectionist.

His father, who owned his own construction company, was a winter-born too and the son (your foreman) grew up in an environment where perfection was driven home to him every day and that the road to success was to be professional about every detail. Now, if you understand your employees' personalities, you could figure out half a dozen ways to smooth out the situation for the men under your foreman, while empowering him. This is especially important if he is a professional, is getting things done, and is not someone that you want to lose. By using the Seasoned Personality concept to better understand your executives and employees, you can delegate the work-load more appropriately according to birth month and their relative attributes.

Let's take one more example. You are a teacher. You play a pivotal role in shaping the future lives of the next generation. Your class is a mix of personalities, with some winter-born and some summer-born. Your view of your students and their performance could be affected by your reaction to their personality types. A simple review of birth months would reveal who possesses the attributes of summer- or winter-born. This would help you understand each student's characteristics and, in turn, assist them better. The job of the teacher is, of course, to get the students to learn and to succeed, not only scholastically, but ultimately in life! So understanding the Seasoned Personality would be valuable.

There are countless situations that I could detail here because there are billions of people on this planet.

Relationships between people are as essential as the air that we breathe. You can't live on this planet without being involved, in some way, with people, unless you hide in some mountains and become a recluse.

What are we all trying to accomplish in life?

Make money? Sure—money is good.

Find our true love? Absolutely—we all want to find that very special person to spend our lives with.

Get a career that we love and that makes us wake up every morning ready to get to work? Yes—we all want to achieve that ideal work environment where our work is our passion.

But what is it that weaves through all of this?

Being HAPPY!

People want to be happy in life. We dream, we work, we get married, we have children, and we aspire to great things because these things make us happy.

People are so focused on being happy these days. Magazines and books are geared to "how to" be happy, make someone happy, live happily and more

Being happy comes from within. By being content with who you are, you can then be happy with others. It doesn't matter what the circumstances may be, when you're at peace with yourself, life seems so much brighter.

The first step to this peace is learning about who *you are.*

Examine your strengths and your weaknesses. Think about factors such as your upbringing, how your parents treated you, your birth order relative to other siblings, the environment where you grew up, and any significant person who influenced you. How did these things affect you?

For the next step, find out about other people's personalities. Understand, and then accept them as who they are, without immediately trying to change them or criticize them for being themselves.

For example, you might find yourself in a situation where you are with someone who is laid back and easy going (summer-born). Yet, you're someone who likes to get things done right away (winter-born). This alone could create friction in the relationship.

What do you do?

You have to be somewhat patient. You can't expect him or her to be like you. They're going to take time to do things in their own time.

That's my third point. You can't expect the other person to *be* like you.

You have heard this truth many times, and it seems to be such a no-brainer. However, we frequently forget this truth and find ourselves tripping up.

We expect other people to treat us the way we treat them. We expect other people to think and feel the way we do. We expect other people to do things the way we do them. And when they don't, we criticize them. At times when understanding is most needed, people fly off the handle, get mad, get upset with one another, or make assumptions about others that are not founded on fact. Remember, if you truly love someone, you also understand that person and have to be able to grant them their right to BE who they are.

We all see the world through our own eyes and per-spective. But in dealing with other people, you must extend your view to see their world and their perspective.

It's not uncommon knowledge that men and women differ sometimes in how they view things in life. For example, when women mention that they have a headache to their husband or boyfriend, they're looking for a way to talk to them about why they have a headache (because of the kid, bad day at work, etc). Men, on the other hand, think there is a problem which they need to solve. Instead of doing the simplest thing in the world and just listening, they all too often advise the woman to "go take an aspirin," only to find out later that their wife has an even worse headache.

How can you be happy?

By *knowing and accepting yourself.*

W E'VE ALL SEEN MOVIES or read stories about people on a downward spiral towards failure, who are taken under the wing of someone who helps them, understands and acknowledges them for *who* they are, instead of criticizing and reminding them about their weaknesses. Suddenly, these people begin to blossom again and can look life straight in the eyes and take it on again.

We all grow a little or a lot, under people who acknowledge us, who encourage and empower by reminding us about our strengths and guide us through our weaknesses.

Let's pay a final visit to the examples in chapter four of this book.

In example #1, what can Jerry do to cope with Chloe? If Jerry understands that his wife is a summer-born and accepts that her tendencies are not the same as his, then he can defuse some of the tension between them by simply giving her more space to be herself. He can clean and organize his closet all he wants, but he doesn't have to expect Chloe's closet to be *like* his. He can organize his home office as he likes, but he shouldn't criticize her because her end of the office is not the same.

Similarly, Chloe, recognizing that her husband is a winter-born and knowing that he is constantly driven, organized and intensely self-demanding, can learn to live with the recognition that he will sometimes be overly demanding, sometimes so driven that she feels micromanaged. By recognizing seasonal attributes, she can learn to accept him, and together they can build stronger bonds based on understanding and not just tolerance.

I am not advocating a relationship that involves compromising oneself or allowing others to go off-track or to engage in self-destructive activities. I am talking about understanding other people and learning to accept them for who they are and then building on that platform.

In example #2, Brett, is a summer-born. He is engaged in a new career that demands tremendous attention to detail and organization, contrary to his relaxed persona. In order for him to continue and succeed as an account representative, he must focus more on getting his paperwork done. He needs to come up with strategies to deal with the administrative end of the job, while still building on his merits and strong qualities. Otherwise, he will very likely find himself looking for a new job that suits his personality. This story happens routinely in the workday setting.

If you were Brett's boss, and you understood the material in this book, how could you help him to be a more effective worker? Understanding winter and summer-born attributes can help answer some of these questions.

In example #3, where Emily goes to the family Thanksgiving dinner, she is faced with what she sees as a grueling task of spending a day with her family. It would behoove her to take a few moments ahead of time to quickly assess her family members' birth months. She might understand them better. Because she understands them, she can grant them the right to be who they are without getting upset around them. As a result, Emily could have a good time at the dinner.

Take a moment to look at the people around you. With the Seasoned Personality concept, you can have better insight. It definitely gives you the base line for somebody's personality. With that accomplished, you can then figure out their strengths and weaknesses. And lastly, you can try to understand them and see where your personality fits into theirs.

I have shared these findings with many of my friends, who have told me that the Seasoned Personality has helped them in their relationships. They had never thought about season of somebody's birthday as a means of insight into personality.

It is my fervent hope that you will benefit as well.

We all know that when we are born into this world, no one walks up to us and hands us a manual of how to understand and live with others successfully. That would be a wonderful manual to receive.

This book is not *the* manual. But it can serve you well as a roadmap, a sort of GPS on the subject of people.

You are surrounded by people born in winter and summer. Gleaning a better understanding of them through this book will help you and them.

Just imagine what it would be like if everyone was born in a winter month. People would always be trying to make everyone measure up to a higher standard.

Maybe it would be better for everyone if we were all born in the summer months. Needless to say, we would all be a lot more relaxed.

In closing, here is a story that demonstrates the domino effect of our actions with other people. It is the story of the farmer who once heard a young boy crying out from a nearby bog. The farmer dropped his tools and ran to the bog. He found a boy, terrified and mired up to his waste in black muck. The farmer saved the boy from what could have been a very slow and horrible death.

The next day, a fancy carriage pulled up to the farmer's sparse home, and an elegantly dressed nobleman stepped out and introduced himself as the father of the boy whom the farmer had saved. He wanted to repay the farmer for saving his son's life, but the farmer refused to accept any payment. Finally the nobleman's son came up to the door, and spotting another boy in the house, he asked if that was the farmer's son. The farmer proudly replied that this was his son indeed. The nobleman proposed to the farmer that he allow him to provide the farmer's son with the same level of education that his own son would have. The farmer agreed to this. The farmer's son attended the very best schools and graduated and became known as the man who discovered penicillin. His name was Sir Alexander Fleming.

Years later, the same nobleman's son (previously saved from the bog) was stricken with pneumonia. What saved his life at that time was penicillin. The name of that nobleman was Lord Randolph Churchill, and his son's name was Sir Winston Churchill.

The moral of the story is that it does matter what you do and say to people. It can in fact make all the difference in the world.

Now that you've read this entire book, try using the Seasoned Personality.

Bibliography

Bolton, Ralph. Personal Interview. 22 Nov. 2008

Gordon, Russell & Masao, Ohmura. "Blood types and athletic performance." *Journal of Psychology* 2002: 161–164.

Kagan, Jerome. The Temperamental Thread: How Genes, Culture, Time and Luck Makes Us Who We Are. Washington, D.C.: Dana press, 2010.

Martin, Jacqueline Briggs. *Snowflake Bentley.* Boston: Houghton Mifflin Co., 1998.

Mitsuhiro Kamata, et al. "Effect of month of birth on personality traits of healthy Japanese." *European Psychiatry* March 2009: 86–90.

Murray, Gregory. *Seasonality, Personality and the Circadian Regulation of Mood.* New York: Nova Science Pub. Inc., 2006.

Schauffler, Haven, ed. *Lincoln's Birthday.* New York: Moffat, Yard and Co., 1914.

Vinogradov, A. E. "Winter-biased birthday theory." Scientometrics. March 1998: 417–420.

Made in the USA
Charleston, SC
17 January 2013